Bugs in Peril

The story of the Simandoa cockroach

This story begins with destruction. The Simandou Range in the Republic of Guinea, beautiful and ecologically diverse, is also rich with minerals like bauxite, iron, and diamonds.

In 2002 Rio Tinto, the second largest mining company in the world, decided to extend their mining operations in Guinea.

Even while recognized as a renowned biodiversity hotspot, Guinea's rainforests are very understudied. To make sure the new mining operations complied with international wildlife laws, Rio Tinto called the organization Consvervation International.

Scientists were sent to the field to assess the biodiversity of the rainforests. This information would then be used to protect the most important areas. These locations included the Pic de Fon Classified Forest in the Simandoa Range, a supposed protected area, now under threat.

Louis M. Roth and Piotr Naskrecki were two entomologists involved in the assessment.

MICROCOSM PUBLISHING is Portland's most diversified publishing house and distributor, with a focus on the colorful, authentic, and empowering. Our books and zines have put your power in your hands since 1996, equipping readers to make positive changes in their lives and in the world around them. Microcosm emphasizes skill-building, showing hidden histories, and fostering creativity through challenging conventional publishing wisdom with books and bookettes about DIY skills, food, bicycling, gender, self-care, and social justice. What was once a distro and record label started by Joe Biel in a drafty bedroom was determined to be *Publishers Weekly*'s fastest-growing publisher of 2022 and #3 in 2023 and 2024, and is now among the oldest independent publishing houses in Portland, OR, and Cleveland, OH. We are a politically moderate, centrist publisher in a world that has inched to the right for the past 80 years.

The scientists worked tirelessly to catalog each and every species they found in Guinea's forests.

A colony of over a thousand Egyptian fruit bats *(Rousettus aegyptiacus)* lived in the cave.

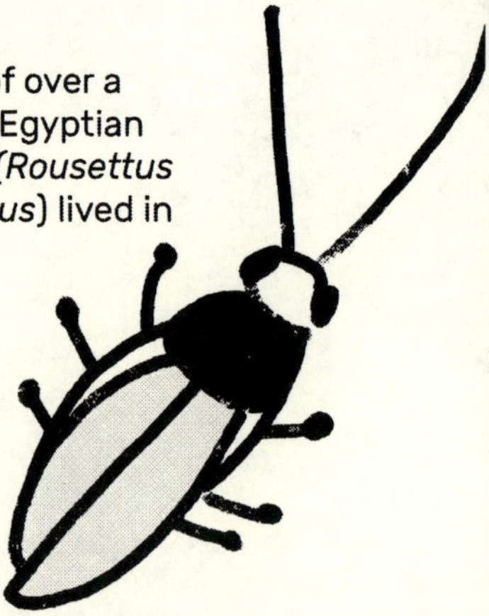

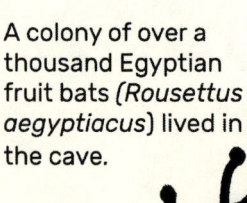

Cave crickets *(Phaeophilacris sp.)* could be found in every nook and cranny of the walls.

Two species of cockroach (*Margattioidea sp.* and *Anapledta sp.*) were found on the ground and walls of the cave.

Neither species have a common name.

Both species were visually described in the journal published about this cave "so they can be recognized again, if collected in the future."

No easily accessible photos exist of either species.

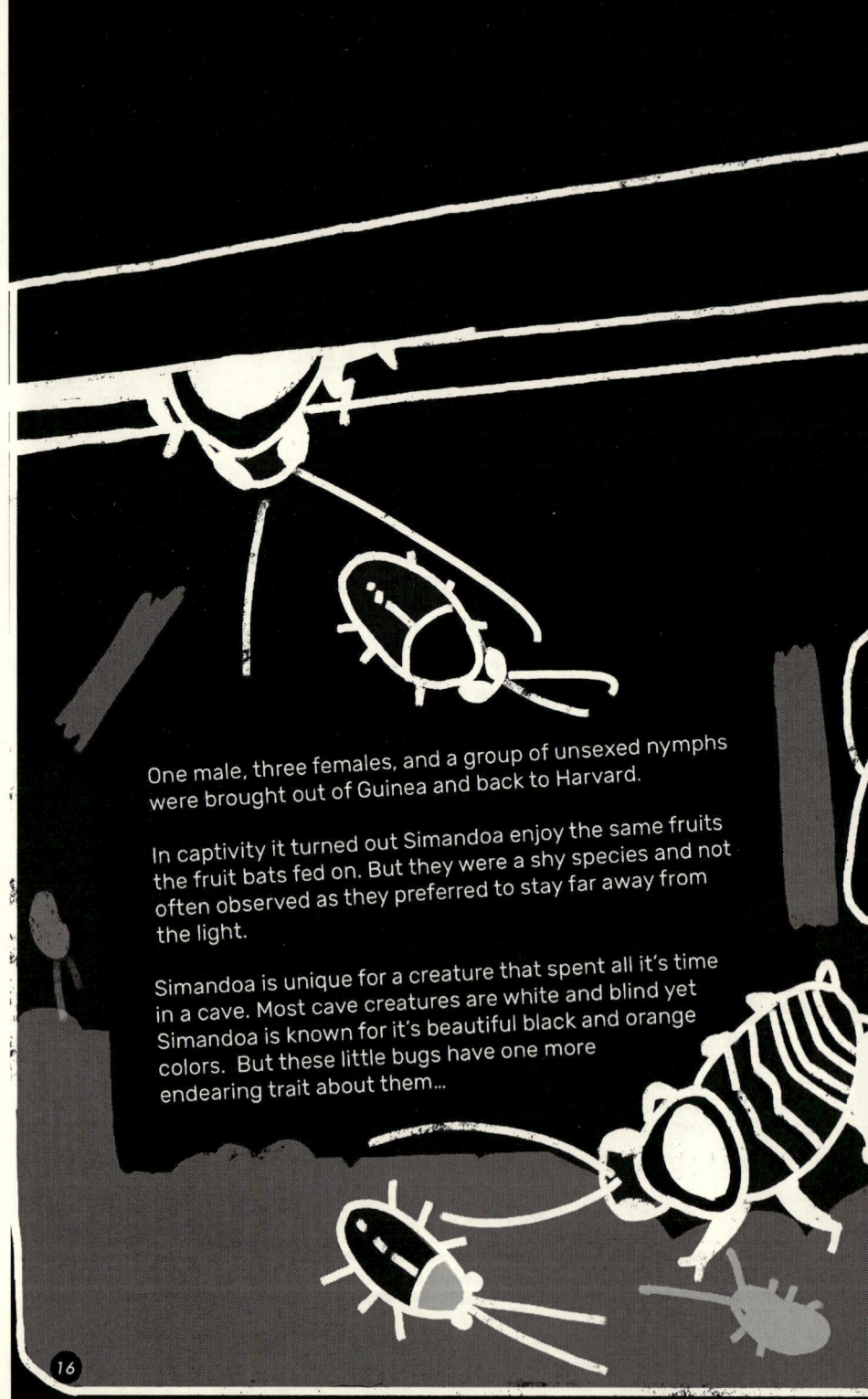

One male, three females, and a group of unsexed nymphs were brought out of Guinea and back to Harvard.

In captivity it turned out Simandoa enjoy the same fruits the fruit bats fed on. But they were a shy species and not often observed as they preferred to stay far away from the light.

Simandoa is unique for a creature that spent all it's time in a cave. Most cave creatures are white and blind yet Simandoa is known for it's beautiful black and orange colors. But these little bugs have one more endearing trait about them...

In June 2004, the pair published in the *Scientific Journal of Orthoptera Research* describing the roaches to science.

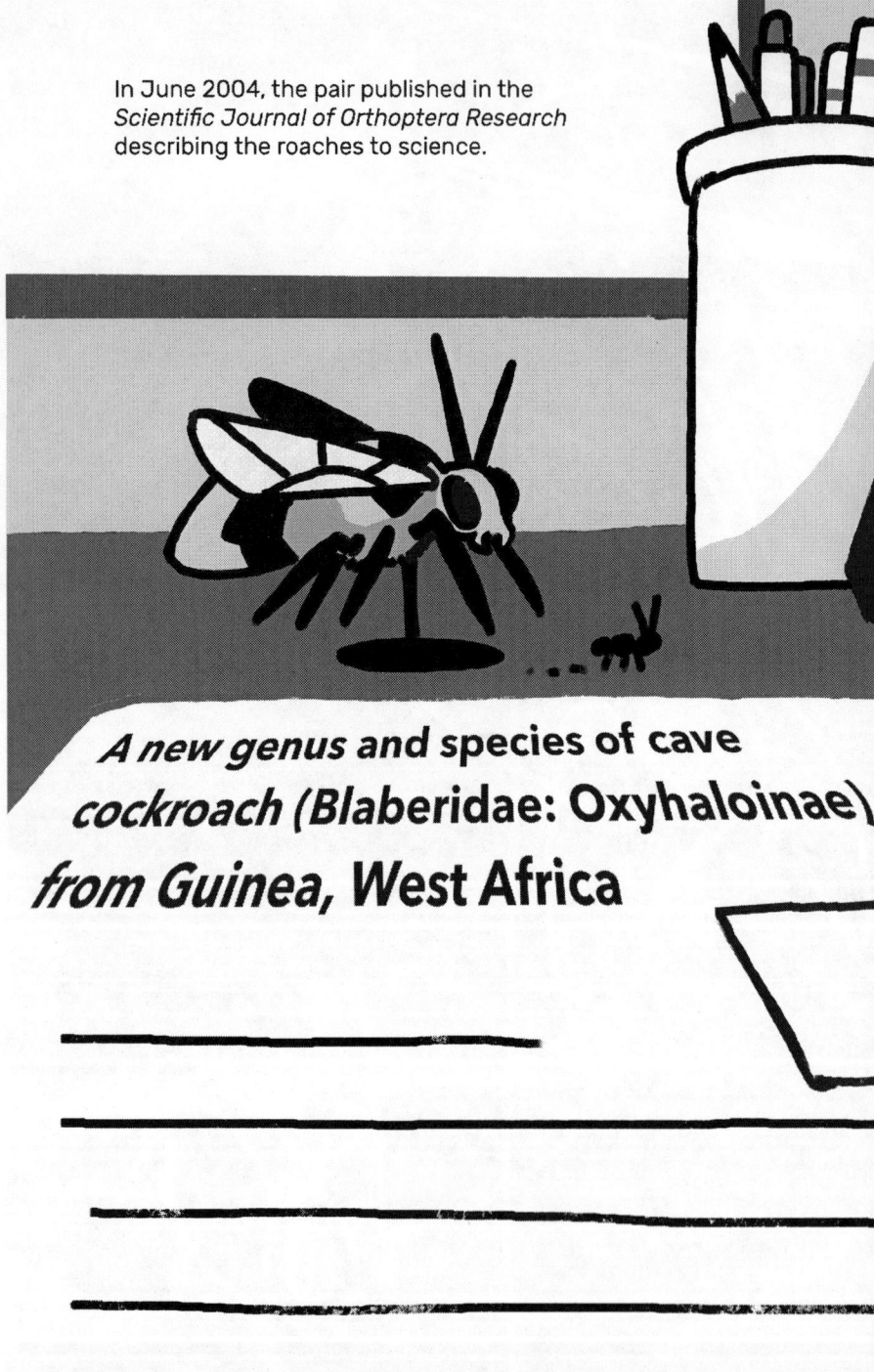

A new genus and species of cave *cockroach (Blaberidae: Oxyhaloinae)* from Guinea, West Africa

It is the document that this project is based on.

It is also the only journal that will ever feature this species.

In the following years the Simandoa mountain range was heavily mined for bauxite and iron.

It was thought that the cave was destroyed during this operation. In reality, the cave existed until at least 2008. It lay only feet from a mining road.

Referencing updated satellite imagery from January of 2024, we can now almost certainly confirm the cave has been destroyed.

Simandoa has never been found anywhere else in the world and is considered extinct in the wild.

A Quick Guide to
Cave Ecosystems

Cave ecosystems are magestic microclimates that we are only now beginning to understand. Scientists are often finding new species that inhabit caves. In some places up to 90% of a cave's species are still unknown to science.

Caves are wet, humid habitats that often hold 100% humidity and cooler temperatures than the surface outside.

Over thousands of years, dripping water causes stalagmites and stalagtites to form, growing approximately one inch per thousand years.

STALAGMITE
Mites crawl up!

STALAGTITE
hang on tight!

Finding nutrients in caves is hard since plants cannot photosynthesize. Inhabitants often rely on outside sources that have found their way into the cave. Storm water, debris, tree roots breaking through the roof, and shelter seeking animals all bring in nutrients.

Bats are the most common outside visitor, with at least 50% of bat species using caves at some point in their life cycle.

While having a bad connotation to their names, bats are our friends! They help keep down mosquito populations and pollinate our crops like agave and durian fruits.

White-Nose Syndrome

Is a fungus currently annhilating bats all over the world. The fungus has even presented an 100% mortality rate in some colonies. This fungus appears white and fuzzy on bats during hibernation. Common effects that may lead to death are restlessness during hibernation leading to starvation, wing damage, loss in temperature regulation, trouble breathing, and dehydration. White-nose syndrome poses no threat to people or non-bat creatures.

If you suspect a bat is sick or died from white-nose syndrome, report it online to your local state wildlife agency.

Please only observe bats from a safe distance. Due to their large colonies, Bats are at higher risk for carrying rabies and other zoonotic diseases. If you are or even suspect you've been bitten by a bat, seek medical treatment immediately.

Since Simandoa's cave was so shallow, it would have been filled with **Troglophiles** ('cave lovers') who, while perferring caves, can survive outside them. It may have also been home to creatures passing seeking shelter from the weather. In Guinea that could have been creatures like leopards, chimpanzees, or even pygmy hippos.

True cave creatures, **Troglobites,** ('cave life') are beings that are entirely adapted to caves and cannot survive outside of a cave.

Adaptations to cave life often involve loss of color, loss of eyes, extended limbs, and long antenna. Troglobites survive off their touch, taste, and smell.

Simandoa is an outlier, and lacks many cave adaptations, like retaining the bright colors of their exoskeleton. For some, this has called into question their status as a true troglobite.

Invertebrates are the most common cave critter. Depending on location and size of cave, there can be an abundance of invertebrate diversity as they fill each niche in the cave ecosystem.

Some creatures often found throughout caves are harvestmen, spiders, cave crickets, millipedes, and of course, roaches.

Stygobite is the aquatic version of a troglobite. A surprising amount of aquatic species have been found in caves, ranging from fish, to crayfish, and even cave clams. The most well known example of a stygobite is the Devils Hole Pupfish, a dark blue fish found in a single limestone cave in Nevada.

Earth is at a perilous moment right now, and we have a duty to our planet, each other, and the creatures that live here to protect it. We must work together to make this home we share a better place for all. Thankfully, no matter who you are or how much you may have to spare, there are many options as to how you can help.

Volunteer
Lending your time to local conservation organizations is the most directly impactful thing you can do to help protect the environment. Look for government initiatives and science led local organizations to volunteer with. If those groups are inaccessible, simply picking up trash can be a great way to start making a difference.

Gardening
Even a few native plants help the local species that depend on them. With that, reducing use of and switching to environmentally friendly pesticides and fungicides is also extremely important. If you lack an outdoor space of your own, dawn a hi-vis jacket and look into guerrilla gardening.

Make sure the species you plant are native directly to your area. Local governmental extensions and colleges may have great resources on local native plants. Avoid commercially available wildflower seed packs in chain stores.

Depending on your state, you may even be able to receive tax write-offs or funding to create native gardens that serve as wildlife habitat.

Many native species can even be found for free in areas unsafe for them, like sidewalks. Apps like **Inaturalist** and **Seek** can be used to identify such plants.
Go ahead, take them home.

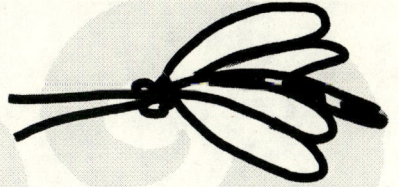

Donating
Just like on the grounds volunteering, funding lets organizations keep doing the good work. If you can't spare cash, offer up your skills instead; whether that be objects to add to a fundraiser, or simply the offer to work pro bono. Local conservation initiatives will put your money to more direct use than massive nonprofits who have access to larger sources of funding.

The Xerces Society is one of the leading and largest insect conservation organizations in the US. Check out their website for even more resources on how you can help.

The protection of the environment is in a tense place right now, but all over the world people are making massive efforts to change the planet for the better. Don't get intimidated by only being able to add a little puzzle piece. A couple of native flowers planted could make the world of difference to species you may never even know exist.

Because the good thing about insects, birds, fish, mammals? If you provide a space for them, they will come.

And in the animal world, word travels fast.

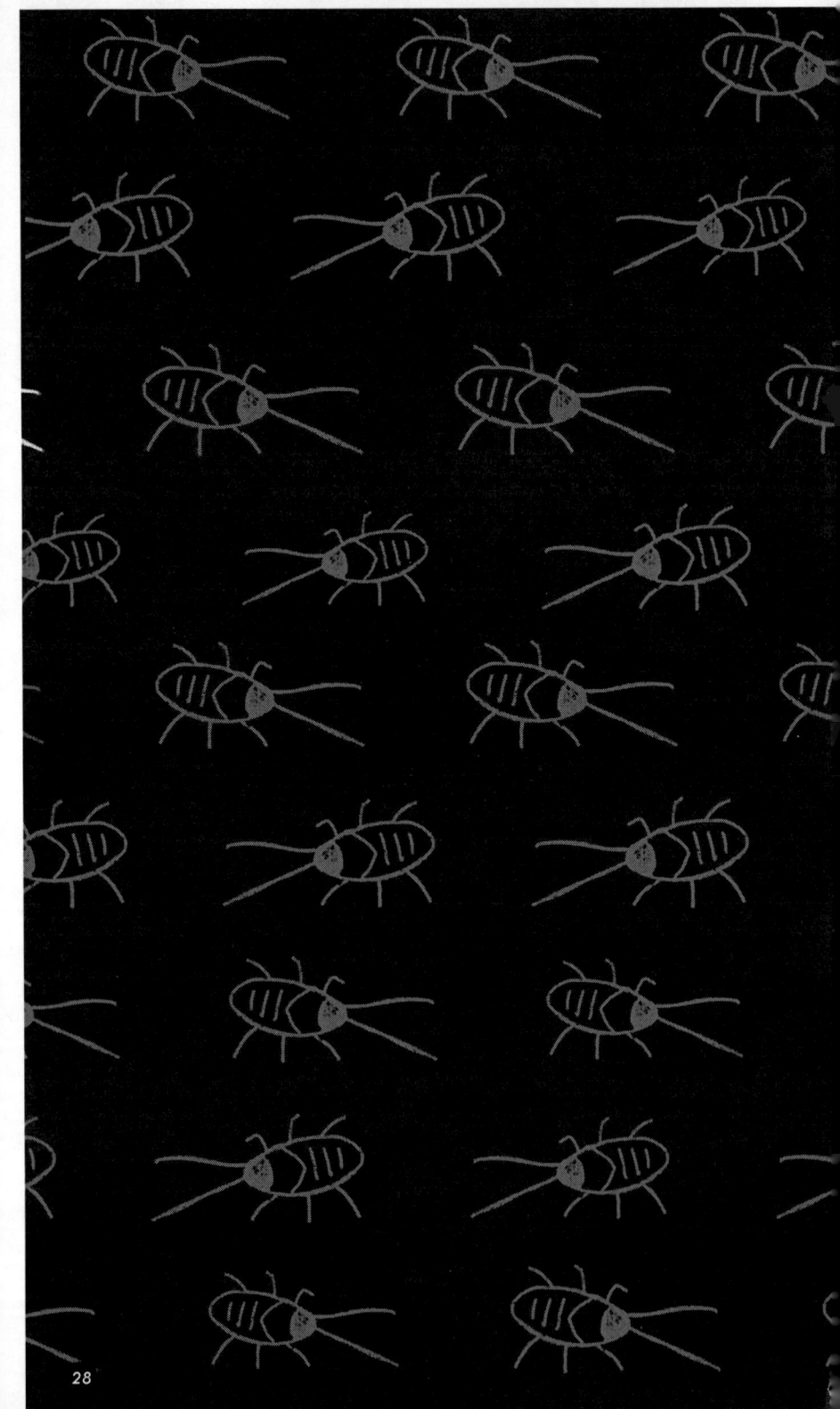

Works cited

Endangered invertebrates – a case for attention to invertebrate conservation. Xerces Society for Invertebrate conservation . (2002, September 27). https://xerces.org/press/endangered-invertebrates-case-for-attention-to-invertebrate-conservation

Premate, E., Borko, Š., Delić, T., Malard, F., Simon, L., & Fišer, C. (2021). Cave amphipods reveal co-variation between morphology and trophic niche in a low-productivity environment. Freshwater Biology, 66(10), 1876–1888. https://doi.org/10.1111/fwb.13797

Roth, L. M., & Naskrecki, P. (2004). A new genus and species of cave cockroach (blaberidae: Oxyhaloinae) from Guinea, West Africa. Journal of Orthoptera Research, 13(1), 57–61. https://doi.org/10.1665/1082-6467(2004)013[0057:angaso]2.0.co;2

Simandou. Global. (n.d.). https://www.riotinto.com/en/operations/projects/simandou

Tanalgo, K. C., Oliveira, H. F. M., & Hughes, A. C. (2022). Mapping global conservation priorities and habitat vulnerabilities for cave-dwelling bats in a Changing World. Science of The Total Environment, 843, 156909. https://doi.org/10.1016/j.scitotenv.2022.156909

U.S. Department of the Interior. (2015, April 10). The biology of Caves. National Parks Service. https://www.nps.gov/ozar/learn/education/cave-biology.htm

White-nose syndrome in bats. Washington Department of Fish & Wildlife. (n.d.). https://wdfw.wa.gov/species-habitats/diseases/bat-white-nose

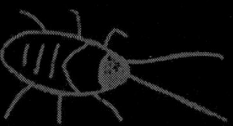

SUBSCRIBE!

For as little as $15/month, you can support a small, independent publisher and get every book that we publish—delivered to your doorstep!

www.Microcosm.pub/BFF